I0426376

Organ Pipe Cactus National Monument

Acoustical Monitoring 2009

Natural Resource Technical Report NPS/NRSS/NRTR—2012/520

Katy Warner
National Park Service
Natural Sounds and Night Skies Division
1201 Oakridge Drive, Suite 100
Fort Collins, CO 80525

January 2012

U.S. Department of the Interior
National Park Service
Natural Resource Stewardship and Science
Fort Collins, Colorado

The National Park Service, Natural Resource Stewardship and Science office in Fort Collins, Colorado publishes a range of reports that address natural resource topics of interest and applicability to a broad audience in the National Park Service and others in natural resource management, including scientists, conservation and environmental constituencies, and the public.

The Natural Resource Technical Report Series is used to disseminate results of scientific studies in the physical, biological, and social sciences for both the advancement of science and the achievement of the National Park Service mission. The series provides contributors with a forum for displaying comprehensive data that are often deleted from journals because of page limitations.

All manuscripts in the series receive the appropriate level of peer review to ensure that the information is scientifically credible, technically accurate, appropriately written for the intended audience, and designed and published in a professional manner.

Data in this report were collected and analyzed using methods based on established, peer-reviewed protocols and were analyzed and interpreted within the guidelines of the protocols.

Views, statements, findings, conclusions, recommendations, and data in this report do not necessarily reflect views and policies of the National Park Service, U.S. Department of the Interior. Mention of trade names or commercial products does not constitute endorsement or recommendation for use by the U.S. Government.

This report is available from the Natural Sounds and Night Skies Division website (http://www.nature.nps.gov/naturalsounds/) and the Natural Resource Publications Management website (http://www.nature.nps.gov/publications/nrpm/).

Please cite this publication as:

Warner, K. 2012. Organ Pipe Cactus National Monument: Acoustical monitoring 2009. Natural Resource Technical Report NPS/NRSS/NRTR—2012/520. National Park Service, Fort Collins, Colorado.

NPS 157/112144, January 2012

Contents

Tables

Figures

Executive Summary

In April of 2009, three acoustical monitoring systems were deployed in Organ Pipe Cactus National Monument (ORPI). The purpose of this monitoring effort was to characterize existing sound levels and estimate natural ambient sound levels in these areas, as well as identify audible sound sources prior to the construction of several Department of Homeland Security Rapid Deployment Towers (RDT) that will be located on or adjacent to ORPI. Towers in remote areas will be powered using solar power with a propane generator as a backup. In order to estimate the noise impacts of operating the RDTs, baseline data from ORPI and additional data on the RDT generators were needed. To meet these objectives, three sound systems ran for 37 days. Two of the monitoring sites were in close proximity to proposed tower sites, and the third site was near Bate Well where Border Patrol had a base camp for the duration of the monitoring effort. Additionally, sound pressure level readings were taken at the site of an existing RDT in Playas, NM. The issue of increased noise is of special interest due to the presence of Sonoran pronghorn in ORPI. This subspecies is federally listed as endangered, and may prefer habitat with lower noise levels (Landon, et al., 2003).

In determining the current conditions of an acoustical environment, it is informative to examine how often sound pressure levels exceed certain values. Table 1 reports the percent of time that measured levels were above four key values. The first value, 35 dBA, is designed to address the health effects of sleep interruption. Recent studies suggest that sound events as low as 35 dB can have adverse effects on blood pressure while sleeping (Haralabidis, 2008). The second value addresses the World Health Organization's recommendations that noise levels inside bedrooms remain below 45 dBA (Berglund et al., 1999). The third value, 52 dBA, is based on the EPA's speech interference level for speaking in a raised voice to an audience at 10 meters. This value addresses the effects of sound on interpretive presentations in parks. The final value, 60 dBA, provides a basis for estimating impacts on normal voice communications at 1 meter. Hikers and visitors viewing scenic vistas in the park would likely be conducting such conversations.

Table 1. Percent time above metrics

Site ID	% Time above sound level: 0700 to 1900				% Time above sound level: 1900 to 0700			
	35 dBA	45 dBA	52 dBA	60 dBA	35 dBA	45 dBA	52 dBA	60 dBA
ORPI001	42.34	8.86	1.67	0.24	22.45	1.51	0.37	0.08
ORPI002	100.00	69.33	0.63	0.06	100.00	87.45	0.56	0.01
ORPI003	23.35	3.22	0.48	0.07	2.43	0.52	0.18	0.04

Table 2 shows results from eight days of off-site listening and visual data analysis for each site. The natural ambient and existing ambient levels are presented. Due to a generator running continuously at ORPI002 (Bates Well/ BP Camp), off-site listening was not conducted. The generator was audible 100% of the time, so the natural ambient level could not be calculated. For ORPI001 and ORPI003, vehicle noise was the largest contributor of extrinsic sounds. During times when extrinsic sounds were not present, ORPI sites were very quiet (minimum recorded decibel levels near 15 dBA). The specifications for the LD 831 and microphone used at these sites indicate that the overall system noise floor is about 17 dBA under specific testing conditions. However, the noise floor for individual units will vary, particularly when subjected to extreme temperature and humidity conditions. It should be noted that due to the influence of the noise floor, measurements approaching this level (between 0 and 3dB above the noise floor) may be slightly higher than their true values.

Table 2. Mean percent time audible for extrinsic sounds and aircraft sounds

Site ID	Site Description	Mean % time audible		Median Existing Ambient (L_{50}) in dBA		Median Natural Ambient (L_{nat}) in dBA	
		All Extrinsic	Aircraft	Day	Night	Day	Night
ORPI001	Cabeza Junction	25.3	5.3	31.2	19.5	29.6	17.5
ORPI002	Bates Well/ BP Camp	100	----	45.3	48.3	**NA**	**NA**
ORPI003	North Boundary	17.8	5.0	25.8	15.0	24.9	14.7

Introduction

A 1998 survey of the American public revealed that 72 percent of respondents thought that providing opportunities to experience natural quiet and the sounds of nature was a very important reason for having national parks, while another 23 percent thought that it was somewhat important (Haas & Wakefield 1998). In another survey specific to park visitors, 91 percent of respondents considered enjoyment of natural quiet and the sounds of nature as compelling reasons for visiting national parks (McDonald et. al 1995). Acoustical monitoring provides a scientific basis for assessing the current status of acoustic resources, identifying trends in resource conditions, quantifying impacts from other actions, assessing consistency with park management objectives and standards, and informing management decisions regarding desired future conditions.

National Park Service Natural Sounds and Night Skies Division

The Natural Sounds and Night Skies Division (NSNSD) helps parks manage sounds in a way that balances access to the park with the expectations of park visitors and the protection of park resources. The NSNSD addresses acoustical issues raised by Congress, NPS Management Policies, and NPS Director's Orders. An important element of this mission is working with the Federal Aviation Administration (FAA) to implement the National Parks Air Tour Management Act. Congress mandated that FAA and NPS jointly develop Air Tour Management Plans (ATMPs) for more than 106 parks where commercial air tours operate. The program also provides technical assistance to parks in the form of acoustical monitoring, data processing, park planning support, and comparative analyses of acoustical environments throughout the national park system.

Soundscape Planning Authorities

The National Park Service Organic Act of 1916 states that the purpose of national parks is "… to conserve the scenery and the natural and historic objects and the wild life therein and to provide for the enjoyment of the same in such manner and by such means as will leave them unimpaired for the enjoyment of future generations." In addition to the NPS Organic Act, the Redwoods Act of 1978 affirmed that, "the protection, management, and administration of these areas shall be conducted in light of the high value and integrity of the National Park System and shall not be exercised in derogation of the values and purposes for which these various areas have been established, except as may have been or shall be directly and specifically provided by Congress."

Direction for management of natural soundscapes[1] is represented in 2006 Management Policy 4.9:

> The Service will restore to the natural condition wherever possible those park soundscapes that have become degraded by unnatural sounds (noise), and will protect natural soundscapes from unacceptable impacts. Using appropriate management planning, superintendents will identify what levels and types of unnatural sound constitute acceptable impacts on park natural soundscapes. The frequencies, magnitudes, and durations of acceptable levels of unnatural sound will vary throughout a park, being

---

[1] The 2006 Management Policy 4.9 and related documents refer to "soundscapes" instead of "acoustic resources." When quoting from this authority, it is advisable to note that the term often refers to resources rather than visitor perceptions.

1

generally greater in developed areas. In and adjacent to parks, the Service will monitor human activities that generate noise that adversely affects park soundscapes [acoustic resources], including noise caused by mechanical or electronic devices. The Service will take action to prevent or minimize all noise that through frequency, magnitude, or duration adversely affects the natural soundscape [acoustic resource] or other park resources or values, or that exceeds levels that have been identified through monitoring as being acceptable to or appropriate for visitor uses at the sites being monitored (NPS 2006a).

It should be noted that "the natural ambient sound level—that is, the environment of sound that exists in the absence of human-caused noise—is the baseline condition, and the standard against which current conditions in a soundscape [acoustic resource] will be measured and evaluated" (NPS 2006b). However, the desired acoustic condition may also depend upon the resources and the values of the park. For instance, "culturally appropriate sounds are important elements of the national park experience in many parks" (NPS 2006b). In this case, "the Service will preserve soundscape resources and values of the parks to the greatest extent possible to protect opportunities for appropriate transmission of cultural and historic sounds that are fundamental components of the purposes and values for which the parks were established" (NPS 2006b).

Study Area

Three acoustical monitoring stations were deployed April – May of 2009. These sites were selected because of their proximity to the proposed DHS RDT tower sites.

Table 3. Site Locations

Site ID	Site Name	Dates Deployed	Vegetation	Elevation	Latitude	Longitude
ORPI001	Cabeza Junction	4/28-6/5/2009	creosote, scattered mesquite	336 m	32.13075	-113.08493
ORPI002	Bates Well	4/28-6/5/2009	creosote, scattered mesquite	407 m	32.16952	-112.95064
ORPI003	North Boundary	4/29-6/5/2009	creosote, mesquite, white bursage	452 m	32.20065	-112.98514

Figure 1. ORPI001, Cabeza Junction.
Site was visible from the Cabeza Junction turn around

Figure 2. ORPI002, Bates Well/ Border Patrol Camp.
We had line of sight to the generator visible in the upper right of this photo (white with red stripe)

Figure 3. ORPI003, Northern Boundary.
Location is very near the proposed Tower 4 site

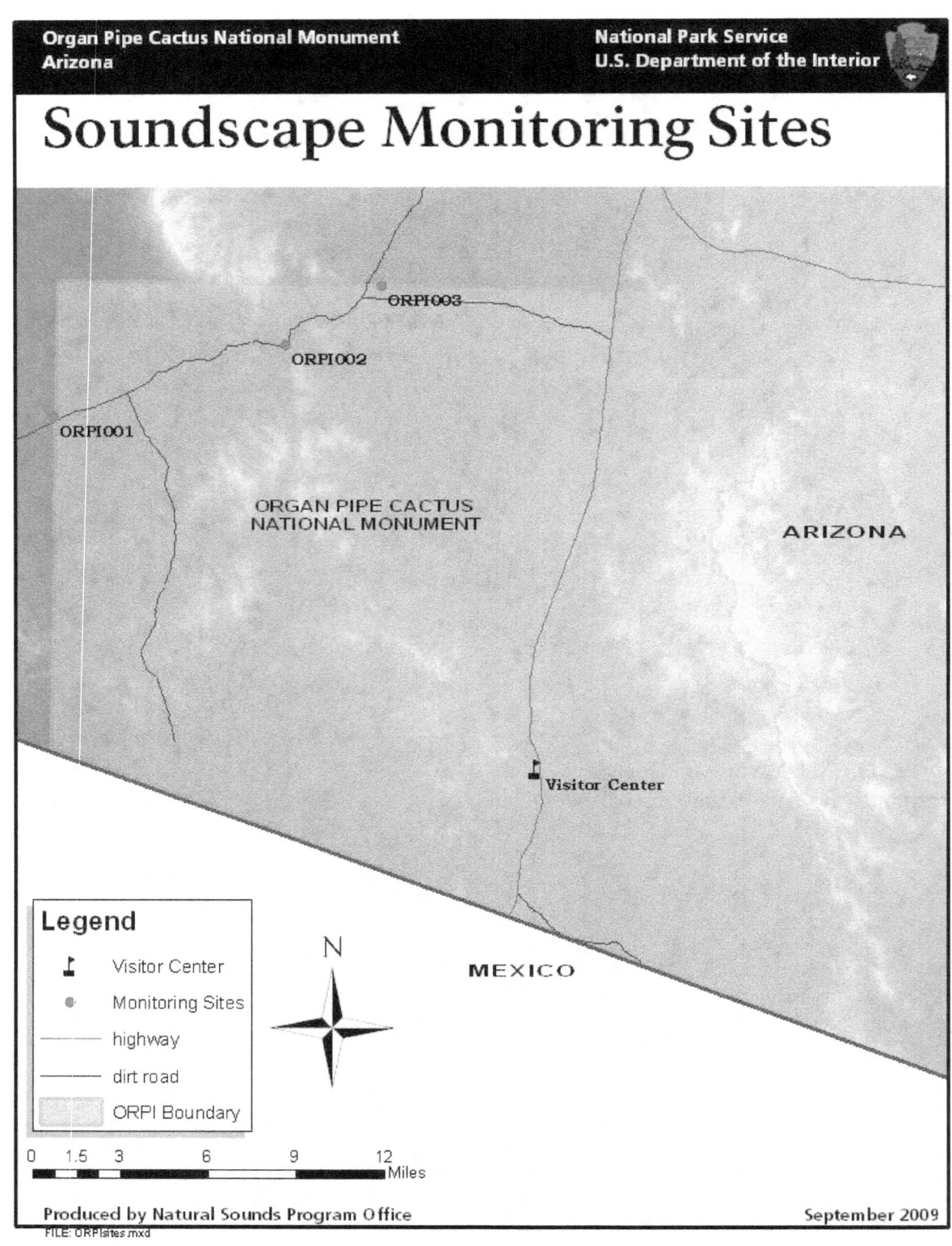

Figure 4. Map of monitoring sites at ORPI

Methods

Automatic Monitoring

Larson Davis 831 sound level meters (SLM) were employed over the thirty day monitoring periods at ORPI. The Larson Davis SLM is a hardware-based, real-time analyzer which constantly records one second sound pressure level (SPL) and 1/3 octave band data, and exports these data to a portable storage device (thumb drive). These Larson Davis-based sites met American National Standards Institute (ANSI) Type 1 standards.

Each Larson Davis sampling station at ORPI consisted of:

- Microphone with environmental shroud
- Preamplifier
- Multiple 12V LiMH rechargeable battery packs
- Anemometer
- MP3 recorder
- Meteorological data logger
- Photo voltaic panels

Each acoustic sampling station collected:

- SPL data in the form of A-weighted decibel readings (dBA) every second
- Continuous digital audio recordings
- One third octave band data every second ranging from 12.5 Hz – 20,000 Hz
- Meteorological data

Off-Site Listening/ Visual Analysis

Visual Analysis was used to analyze ORPI001 and ORPI003 since there were few enough sound sources to easily distinguish them visually. For each monitoring site, Natural Sounds and Night Skies Division (NSNSD) staff visually analyzed a subset of SPL samples (eight days) in order to identify durations of audible sound sources. Audio samples were employed to confirm identification. The total percent time extrinsic sounds were audible was then used to calculate the natural ambient sound level for each hour. Bose Quiet Comfort Noise Canceling headphones were used for off-site audio playback to minimize limitations imposed by the office acoustic environment.

On-Site Listening

On-site listening is the practice of placing an observer near the acoustical monitoring station with a handheld personal digital assistant (PDA). The observer listens for a designated period of time (in this case, one hour), and identifies all sound sources and their durations. On-site listening takes full advantage of human binaural hearing capabilities, and closely matches the experience of park visitors. Logistic constraints prevent comprehensive sampling by this technique, but selective samples of on-site listening provide a basis for relating the results of off-site listening to the probable auditory perception of events by park visitors and wildlife. On-site listening sessions are also an excellent screening tool for parks initiating acoustic environment studies.

They produce an extensive inventory of sound sources, require little equipment or training, and can help educate park staff and volunteers.

Thus, periods of on-site listening were conducted in order to discern the type, timing, and duration during sound-level data collection at ORPI. As recommended by NSNSD protocol (NPS 2005) these sessions generally began at the top of an hour and lasted for one hour. Staff recorded the beginning and ending times of all audible sound sources using custom-designed PDA software. These on-site listening sessions provided the basis for the calculation of metrics including the period of time between noise events (average noise free interval [NFI]), percent time each sound source was audible, and maximum, minimum, and mean length (in seconds) of sound source events.

Calculation of Metrics

The current status of the acoustical environment can be characterized by spectral measurements, durations, and overall sound levels (intensities). The NSNSD uses descriptive figures and metrics to interpret these characteristics. Two fundamental descriptors are existing ambient (L_{50}) and natural ambient (L_{nat}) sound levels. These are both examples of exceedence levels, where each L_x value refers to the sound pressure levels that is exceeded x% of the time. The L_{50} represents the median sound pressure level, and is comprised of spectra (in dB) drawn from a full dataset (removing data with wind speed > 5m/s to eliminate error from microphone distortion.). The natural ambient (L_{nat}) is an estimate of what the ambient level for a site would be if all extrinsic or anthropogenic sources were removed. Unlike the existing ambient, the natural ambient is comprised of spectra drawn from a subset of the original data.

For a given hour (or other specified time period), L_{nat} is calculated to be the decibel level exceeded x percent of the time, where x is defined by the equation:

$$x = \frac{100 - P_H}{2} + P_H ,$$

and P_H is the percentage of samples containing extrinsic or anthropogenic sounds for the hour. For example, if human caused sounds are present 30% of the hour, x = 65, and the L_{nat} is equal to the L_{65}, or the level exceeded 65% of the time. To summarize and display these data, the median of the hourly L_{nat} values for the daytime hours (0700-1900) and the median of the hourly L_{nat} values for the nighttime (1900-0700) are displayed in Figure 5, Figure 6,

Figure 7, and Table 9 in the results section. Additionally, these figures separate the data into 33 one-third octave bands. For further explanation of these metrics, and examples of their interpretation, see the section on Metrics in the Results section below.

Results

Onsite Listening

Table 4 and Table 5 display the results of on-site listening sessions. Each audible sound source is listed in the first column. Percent time audible, or PA, is the second column. The third column, Max Event, reports the maximum event length among the sessions for each sound source. Likewise, Mean Event and Min Event columns report the mean and minimum length of events. SD reports the standard deviation among event lengths, and the Count column reports the number of times that each sound source was audible. Max Event, Mean Event, Min Event, and SD Event are reported in seconds. The last row in the table, noise free interval (NFI), is a metric which describes the length of time between extrinsic or human-caused events when only natural sounds were audible. NFI is also reported in seconds. These on-site listening tables are essentially a sound inventory of each site. They reveal the sounds one is likely to hear at or near this location.

Table 4. Summary of on-site audible sound sources for ORPI001 n=2 hour-long sessions. Events are measured in minutes: seconds.

Sound Source Description	PA (%)	Max Event	Mean Event	Min Event	SD Event	Count
Jet	8	2:11	1:21	0:09	0:47	7
Jet, Military	11	6:54	2:44	0:18	2:38	5
Vehicle	30	14:15	4:03	0:48	5:27	9
People	5	1:33	0:24	0:05	0:23	16
People, Voices	8	5:02	4:35	4:08	0:38	2
Non-natural Unknown	38	7:37	2:42	0:06	2:14	17
Wind	50	6:19	2:37	0:07	1:54	23
Bird	3	1:18	0:15	0:01	0:21	13
Reptile	1	0:49	0:16	0:02	0:19	5
Insect	69	29:29	4:23	0:18	6:38	19
All Aircraft	19.3					
All Road Vehicles	30.3					
All Non-natural Sources	67.6					
All Natural Sources	87.5					
Noise Free Interval	57.1	1,111	242	1	335	17

Off-Site Data Analysis

In determining the current conditions of an acoustical environment, it is important to examine how often sound pressure levels exceed certain values. Table 6 reports the percent of time that measured levels were above four key values. The top value in each split-cell focuses on frequencies affected by transportation noise whereas the lower values use the conventional full frequency range. The first, 35 dBA is designed to address the health effects of sleep interruption. Recent studies suggest that sound events as low as 35 dB can have adverse effects on blood pressure while sleeping (Haralabidis, 2008). The second value addresses the World Health Organization's recommendations that noise levels inside bedrooms remain below 45 dBA (Berglund et al., 1999). The third value, 52 dBA, is based on the EPA's speech interference threshold for speaking in a raised voice to an audience at 10 meters. This threshold addresses the effects of sound on interpretive presentations in parks. The final value, 60 dBA, provides a basis

9

for estimating impacts on normal voice communications at 1 meter. Hikers and visitors viewing scenic vistas in the park would likely be conducting such conversations.

Table 5. Summary of on-site audible sound sources for ORPI003 n = 3 hour-long sessions. Events are measured in minutes : seconds.

Sound Source Description	PA	Max Event	Mean Event	Min Event	SD Event	Count
Jet, Military	13	4:42	1:30	0:06	1:21	16
Vehicle	1	1:37	0:52	0:07	1:04	2
Portable Audio Devices	0	0:02	0:02	0:02	0:01	1
Non-natural Unknown	0	0:46	0:46	0:46	0:01	1
Wind	1	0:59	0:28	0:11	0:27	3
Bird	28	15:57	0:45	0:01	2:03	68
Reptile	1	0:53	0:28	0:03	0:35	2
Insect	66	59:58	59:50	59:41	0:12	2
All Aircraft	13.3					
All Road Vehicles	1					
All Non-natural Sources	14.7					
All Natural Sources	72.2					
Noise Free Interval	85.7	46:27	7:43	0:04	14:01	20

Table 6. Percent time above metrics

Site ID	Frequency (Hz)	% Time above sound level: 0700 to 1900 hours				% Time above sound level: 1900 to 0700 hours			
		35 dBA	45 dBA	52 dBA	60 dBA	35 dBA	45 dBA	52 dBA	60 dBA
ORPI001	20-800[1]	35.48	2.75	0.48	0.11	18.22	1.00	0.26	0.05
	12.5-20,000[2]	42.34	8.86	1.67	0.24	22.45	1.51	0.37	0.08
ORPI002	20-800	100.00	55.10	0.25	0.03	100.00	85.12	0.15	0.00
	12.5-20,000	100.00	69.33	0.63	0.06	100.00	87.45	0.56	0.01
ORPI003	20-800	17.98	1.34	0.24	0.05	1.93	0.38	0.08	0.02
	12.5-20,000	23.35	3.22	0.48	0.07	2.43	0.52	0.18	0.04

1. The top value in each cell focuses on frequencies affected by transportation, which approximately correspond to 100-800 hertz. This range does not correspond to a specific vehicle or type of transportation.
2. The bottom value in each cell uses the full frequency spectrum, from 12.5-20,000 hertz.

Audibility

Table 7 and Table 8 show the mean percentage of time that certain sound sources were audible based on eight days of visual analysis. At ORPI001 and ORPI003 the most pervasive non-natural sound source was vehicle noise. Off-site listening was not conducted for ORPI002, because exploratory analysis revealed that the generator ran continuously for the entire monitoring period. Therefore, non-natural sound was present at ORPI002 100% of the time.

Table 7. Mean percent time audible for each sound source at ORPI001

sound source	07-18h	19h-06h	08-15h	16-07h	24 hrs
Jet	6.6	3.9	8.4	3.6	5.2
Non-natural other	0	0.2	0	0.1	0.1
Truck	11	28.4	12.2	23.4	19.7
ATV	0	0.5	0	0.4	0.2
Non-natural unknown	0	0.2	0	0.1	0.1
Wind	58	13.4	55.8	25.6	35.7
Rain	0.6	1	0.9	0.8	0.8
People	0.4	0.2	0.6	0.2	0.3
Aircraft	6.6	3.9	8.4	3.6	5.2
Total Vehicle Noise	11	28.7	12.2	23.7	19.9
Total Non-Natural	17.6	32.9	20.7	27.6	25.3

Table 8. Mean percent time audible for each sound source at ORPI003

Sound Source	07-18h	19h-06h	08-15h	16-07h	24 hrs
Jet	7.7	3.5	10.8	3	5.6
Helicopter	0.3	0.1	0.4	0.1	0.3
Vehicle	5.8	13.7	3.1	13	9.7
Truck	1.7	2.6	1.8	2.3	2.1
Non-Natural Unknown	0	0.2	0	0.1	0.1
Wind	43.7	18.1	44.4	24.2	30.9
Rain	3.3	2.2	4.8	1.7	2.8
Total Aircraft	8.1	3.6	11.3	3.2	5.9
Total Vehicles	7.5	16.2	4.9	15.3	11.9
Total Non-Natural	15.4	20.1	16	18.6	17.8

Metrics

In order to determine the effect extrinsic noise audibility has on the acoustical environment, it is useful to examine the median hourly exceedence metrics. In Figure 5, Figure 6, and Figure 7, the dB levels for 33 one-third octave band frequencies over the day and night periods are shown. The grayed area represents sound levels outside of the typical range of human hearing. The exceedence levels (L_x) are also shown for each one-third octave band. They represent the dB exceeded x percent of the time. For example, L_{90} is the dB that has been exceeded 90% of the time, and only the quietest 10% of the sample can be found below this point. On the other hand, the L_{10} is the dB that has been exceeded 10% of the time, and 90% of the measurements are quieter than the L_{10}. The bold portion of the column represents the difference between L_{50} (existing ambient) and L_{nat} (natural ambient). The height of this bold portion is a measure of the contribution of anthropogenic noise to the existing ambient sound levels at this site. The size of this portion of the column is directly related to the percent time that human caused sounds are audible. When bold portions of the column do not appear the natural and existing ambient levels were either very close to each other were or equal.

L_{nat} and L_{50} are bordered above by L_{10} and below by L_{90}, which essentially mark the median, maximum, and minimum sounds pressure levels over the 30 day monitoring period. The typical frequency levels for transportation, conversation and songbirds are presented on the figure as examples for interpretation of the data. These ranges are estimates and are not vehicle-, species, or habitat-specific. It can be useful to review each one third octave band on these figures to adequately predict the audibility of one sound or the masking of another. For example, you will notice bird sounds and transportation noise are audible at different frequency spectrums. There may be times when transportation sounds were louder than the bird sounds; however the bird sounds would not be masked because their song is audible at a different frequency. However, if two sounds are within the similar or overlapping frequency ranges and one sound is louder than the other, then you can begin to predict when sounds are going to be masked.

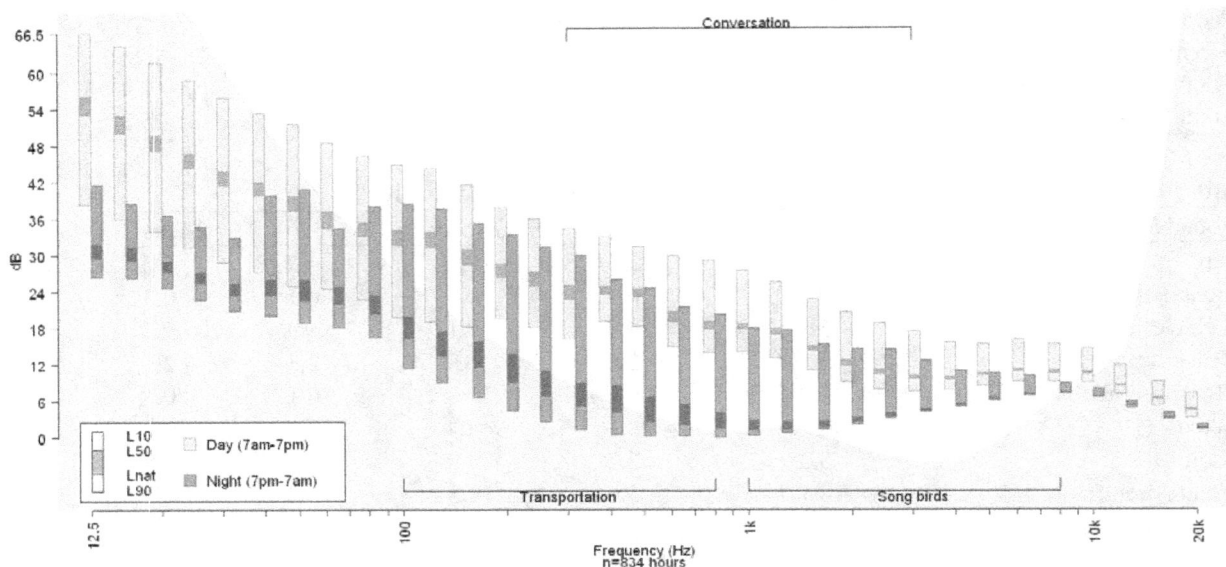

Figure 5. Day and night dB levels for 33 one-third octave bands at ORPI001

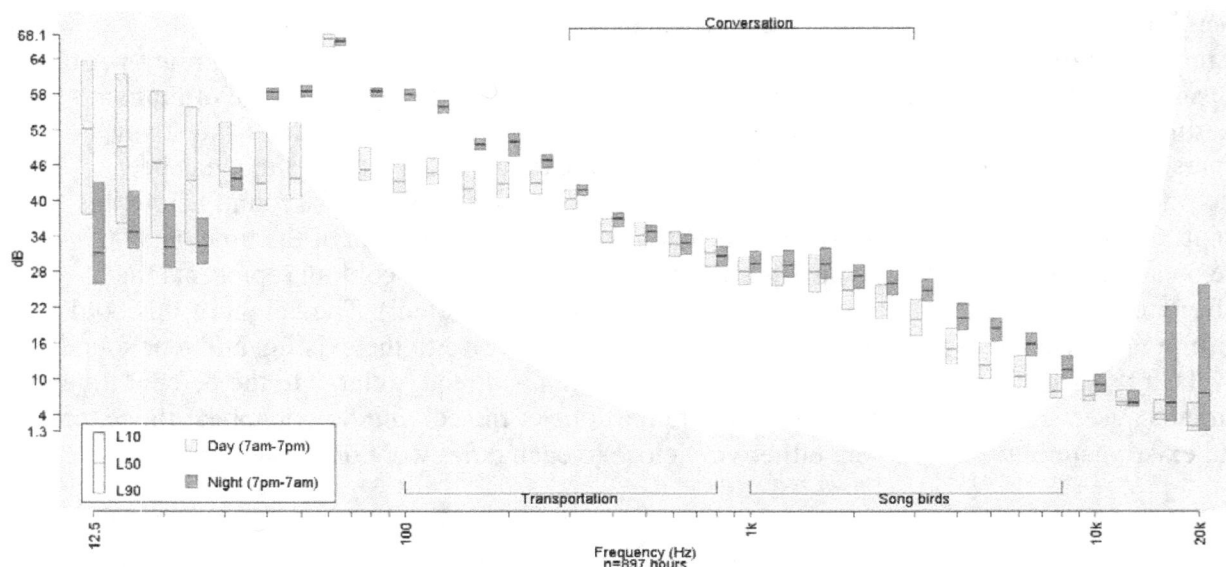

Figure 6. Day and night dB levels for 33 one-third octave bands at ORPI002.
Note: Lnat was not possible to calculate due to constant generator noise.

12

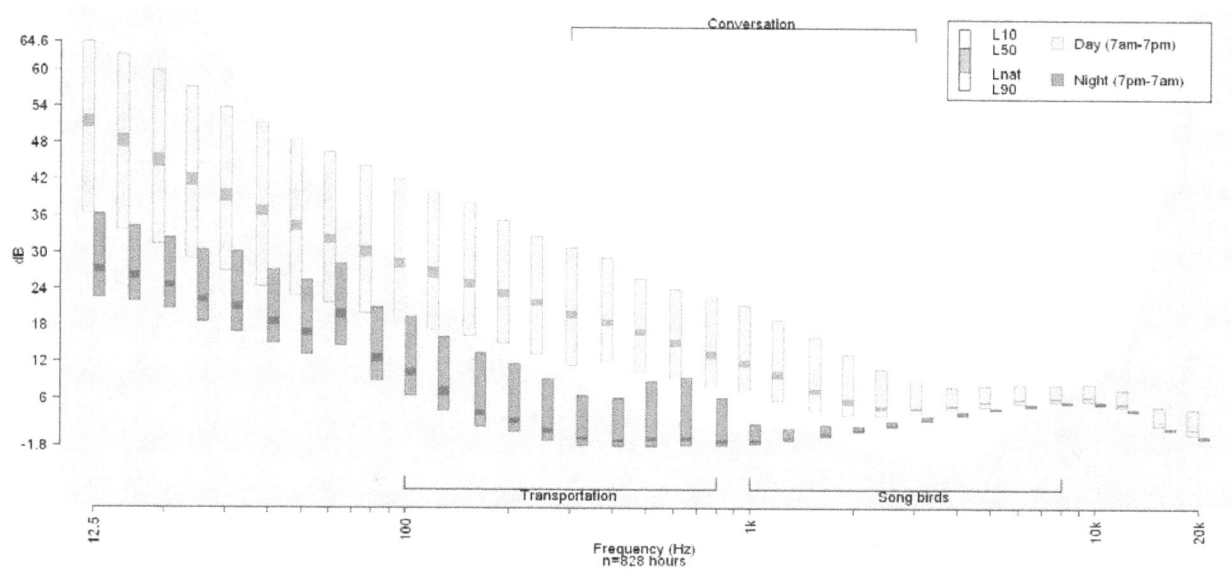

Figure 7. Day and night dB levels for 33 one-third octave bands at ORPI003

Table 9 reports the L_{90}, L_{nat}, L_{50}, and L_{10} values for the sites measured in ORPI. The top value in each cell focuses on frequencies affected by transportation noise whereas the lower values use the conventional full frequency range. As mentioned earlier, it was not possible to calculate the L_{nat} for ORPI002, due to the generator being audible 100% of the time.

Table 9. Exceedence levels for existing conditions

Site	Frequency (Hz)	Exceedence levels (dBA): 0700 to 1900 hours				Exceedence levels (dBA): 1900 to 0700 hours			
		L_{90}	L_{nat}	L_{50}	L_{10}	L_{90}	L_{nat}	L_{50}	L_{10}
ORPI001	20-800	22.0	27.5	29.7	38.3	7.1	10.7	14.8	33.0
	12.5-20,000	24.9	29.6	31.2	41.0	16.0	17.5	19.5	34.1
ORPI002	20-800	44.3	NA	45.0	46.0	47.3	NA	47.9	48.6
	12.5-20,000	44.6	NA	45.3	46.6	47.6	NA	48.3	49.0
ORPI003	20-800	16.5	23.4	24.4	35.0	4.6	6.6	7.6	16.7
	12.5-20,000	19.5	24.9	25.8	36.4	14.3	14.7	15.0	19.2

Discussion

The purpose of this study was to conduct acoustical monitoring at Organ Pipe Cactus National Monument (ORPI) in order to determine current ambient conditions. Monitoring results were intended to give the park baseline information as well as inform management decisions. Sound pressure level, wind speed data, and continuous audio were collected. Additionally, attended logging sessions were conducted at ORPI001 and ORPI003.

Data were gathered from three sites starting the end of April and running through early June of 2009. The sites of ORPI001 and ORPI003 were selected because of their proximity to proposed DHS Rapid Deployment Towers (RDTs) that will be located on or adjacent to ORPI. ORPI002 was located at the current Border Patrol camp, where their facilities were powered using Magnum MMG50 and Magnum MMG25 generators. Generator noise was audible 100% of the time during the 37-day monitoring period at ORPI002. Given the mobile nature of the BP camp, the noise impacts from the generators will accompany the camp in the event that it relocates in the future. The proposed RDTs in remote areas will also be powered using a generator, at least part of the time.

At all three sites, BP activities accounted for the majority of human-caused sounds. The constant generator noise at ORPI002 dominated the soundscape, and was audible 100% of the time. BP trucks idled for 30 minutes to 4.5 hours daily near ORPI001, and on average vehicle noise was audible 19.9% of the time at this site. In general, vehicle noise sounded more distant at ORPI003, and was audible an average of 11.9% of the time. In addition to vehicle noise, jet overflights were audible approximately 5-6% of the time at ORPI001 and ORPI003. Due to limited access to the areas where monitoring sites were located, very few other human-caused sounds were audible.

In addition to the extrinsic sound sources at ORPI, many intrinsic sounds were recorded. Bird and insect sounds were recorded at all sites, as well as the sounds of wind, rain, and thunderstorms. At ORPI001 many birds were present, including ravens and curve-billed thrashers. Despite the generator noise at ORPI002, this site had some interesting results. In Figure 6, the highest two 1/3-octave frequency bands show a significant SPL increase for the nighttime hours (in purple). These high frequency sounds were not nearly as prevalent at the other sites (Figure 5 & Table 7). Bat activity is the most likely source of these sounds, based on the time of day, the high frequency of the sounds, and the habitat. At ORPI003 (the quietest of the three sites) we captured clear recordings of coyotes howling, and an elf owl calling at night. These were just a handful of the many natural sounds that create the acoustical environment at Organ Pipe Cactus National Monument, and contribute to the natural ambient sound levels at each site.

Acoustic monitoring not only allows us to gain insight into biological activity, but also allows us to determine the prevalence of extrinsic noise, and consider how it may affect the visitor experience and wildlife activity within the park. The audibility of human-caused sounds varied greatly among the three sites at ORPI. Over all hours of the day, human-caused sounds were audible 17.8% at ORPI003, 25.3% at ORPI001, and 100% of the time at ORPI002. Based on on-site listening, the mean noise free interval (time between human-caused noise events) ranged from four minutes and 2 seconds at ORPI001 to seven minutes and 43 seconds at ORPI003.

Literature Cited

Berglund, B., Lindvall, T. and Schwela, D.H (Eds.). 1999. HWO. Guidelines for community noise. World Health Organization, Geneva.

Haas, G.E., & Wakefield, T.J. 1998. National parks and the American public: A national public opinion survey on the national park system. Washington D.C. and Fort Collins, CO.: National Parks and Conservation Association and Colorado State University.

Haralabidis Alexandros S., et. al. 2008. "Acute effects of night-time noise exposure on blood pressure in populations living near airports" European Heart Journal Advance Access. Published online February 12, 2008.

Landon, D.M., Krauseman, P.R., Koenen, K.K.G., & Harris, L.K. 2003. Pronghorn use of areas with varying sound pressure levels. The Southwestern Naturalist 48:725-728.

McDonald, C. D., Baumgarten, R. M., and Iachan, R. 1995. Aircraft management studies: National Park Service Visitors Survey. HMMH Report No. 290940.12; NPOA Report No. 94-2, National Park Service, U.S. Department of the Interior.

National Park Service. 2005. Acoustic and Soundscape Studies in National Parks: Draft. Fort Collins, CO: NPS Natural Sounds and Night Skies Division.

National Park Service. 2006a. Management Policy 4.9: Soundscape Management.

National Park Service. 2006b. Management Policy 8.2.3: Use of Motorized Equipment.

Glossary of Acoustical Terms

Acoustical Environment
The actual physical sound resources, regardless of audibility, at a particular location.

Amplitude
The instantaneous magnitude of an oscillating quantity such as sound pressure. The peak amplitude is the maximum value.

Audibility
The ability of animals with normal hearing, including humans, to hear a given sound. Audibility is affected by the hearing ability of the animal, the masking effects of other sound sources, and by the frequency content and amplitude of the sound.

dBA
A-weighted decibel. A-Weighted sum of sound energy across the range of human hearing. Humans do not hear well at very low or very high frequencies. Weighting adjusts for this.

Decibel
A logarithmic measure of acoustic or electrical signals. The formula for computing decibels is: 10(Log10(sound level/reference sound level)). 0 dB represents the lowest sound level that can be perceived by a human with healthy hearing. Conversational speech is about 65 dB.

Diel
A 24-hour period usually consisting of a day and the adjoining night.

Extrinsic Sound
Any sound not forming an essential part of the park unit, or a sound originating from outside the park boundary.

Frequency
The number of times per second that the sine wave of sound repeats itself. It can be expressed in cycles per second, or Hertz (Hz). Frequency equals Speed of Sound/ Wavelength.

Hearing Range (frequency)
By convention, an average, healthy, young person is said to hear frequencies from approximately 20Hz to 20000 Hz.

Hertz
A measure of frequency, or the number of pressure variations per second. A person with normal hearing can hear between 20 Hz and 20,000 Hz.

Human-Caused Sound
Any sound that is attributable to a human source.

Intrinsic sound

A sound which belongs to a park by its very nature, based on the park unit purposes, values, and establishing legislation. The term "intrinsic sounds" has replaced "natural sounds" in order to incorporate both cultural and historic sounds as part of the acoustic environment of a park.

Listening Horizon
The range or limit of one's hearing capabilities. Just as smog limits the visual horizon, so noise limits the acoustic horizon.

L_{eq}
Energy Equivalent Sound Level. The level of a constant sound over a specific time period that has the same sound energy as the actual (unsteady) sound over the same period.

L_x
A metric used to describe acoustic data. It represents the level of sound exceeded x percent of the time during the given measurement period.

Masking
The process by which the threshold of audibility for a sound is raised by the presence of another sound.

Noise-Free Interval
The period of time between noise events (not silence).

Noise
Sound which is unwanted, either because of its effects on humans, its effect on fatigue or malfunction of physical equipment, or its interference with the perception or detection of other sounds (Source: McGraw Hill Dictionary of Scientific and Technical Terms).

Off-site Listening
The systematic identification of sound sources using digital recordings previously collected in the field.

Sound Level Floor (Noise Floor)
The lowest amplitude measurable by sound monitoring equipment.

NPS 157/112144, January 2012